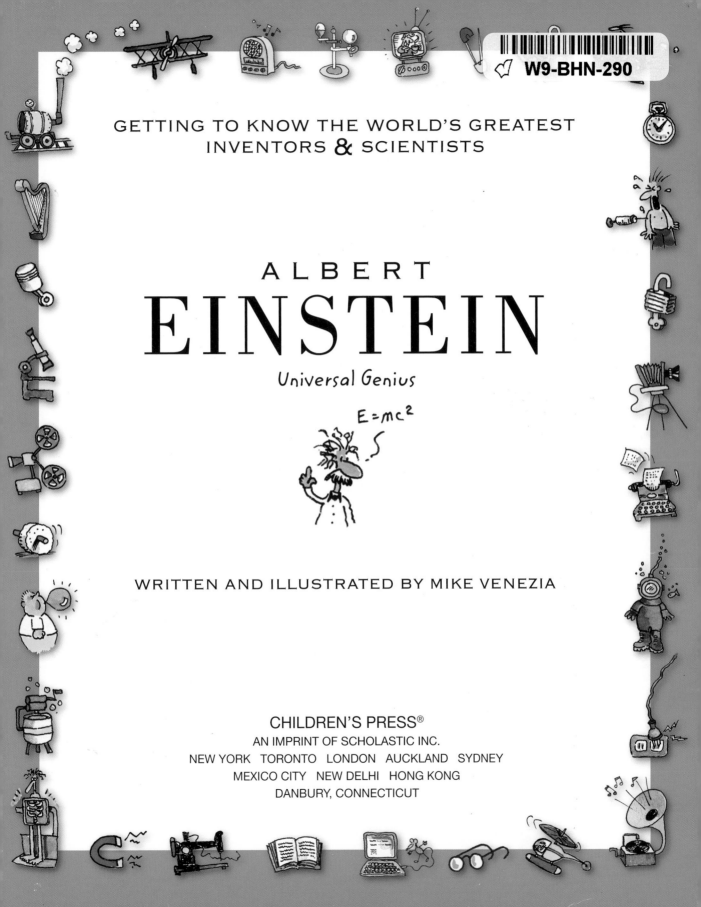

GETTING TO KNOW THE WORLD'S GREATEST
INVENTORS **&** SCIENTISTS

A L B E R T
EINSTEIN

Universal Genius

$E = mc^2$

WRITTEN AND ILLUSTRATED BY MIKE VENEZIA

CHILDREN'S PRESS®
AN IMPRINT OF SCHOLASTIC INC.
NEW YORK   TORONTO   LONDON   AUCKLAND   SYDNEY
MEXICO CITY   NEW DELHI   HONG KONG
DANBURY, CONNECTICUT

To my three Cosmic kids—Mike and Liz Weiler and Mike V.

Reading Consultant: Nanci R. Vargus, Ed.D., Assistant Professor, School of Education, University of Indianapolis

Content Consultant: Joyce Bedi, Senior Historian, Lemelson Center for the Study of Invention and Innovation, National Museum of American History, Smithsonian Institution

Photographs © 2008: AIP Emilio Segrè Visual Archives/Austrian National Library, Vienna: 3; Alamy Images/The Print Collector: 19; Corbis Images: 7, 26, 30 bottom, 30 top, 31 (Bettmann), 15 (Grand Tour), 10 (Tom Grill), 29 (Nagasaki Atomic Bomb Museum/epa), 28 (Underwood & Underwood); ETH-Bibliothek Zurich, Image Archive: 16; The Albert Einstein Archives/The Hebrew University of Jerusalem, Israel: 14, 17, 22; The Granger Collection, New York: 9, 20 (Ullstein Bild), 11, 18.

Colorist for illustrations: Andrew Day

Library of Congress Cataloging-in-Publication Data

Venezia, Mike.
  Albert Einstein : universal genius / written and illustrated by Mike Venezia.
    p. cm. — (Getting to know the world's greatest inventors and scientists)
  Includes index.
  ISBN-13: 978-0-531-14975-1 (lib. bdg.) 978-0-531-22206-5 (pbk.)
  ISBN-10: 0-531-14975-7 (lib. bdg.)   0-531-22206-3 (pbk.)
  1. Einstein, Albert, 1879-1955—Juvenile literature. 2. Physicists—Biography—Juvenile literature. I. Title. II. Series.
  QC16.E5V46 2008
  530.092—dc22
  [B]
                   2008002307

1 2 3 4 5 6 7 8 9 10 R 18 17 16 15 14 13 12 11 10 09

Albert Einstein was born in Ulm, Germany, on March 14, 1879. Albert solved some of the greatest mysteries of the universe. Scientists, as well as everyday people, were fascinated with Albert Einstein and his brilliant theories. During his lifetime, Albert became so popular that he could be considered the first science superstar!

Albert Einstein's most important ideas had to do with **physics**. Physics is the study of **matter** and energy. It includes the areas of motion, electricity, light, sound, and **magnetism**. Albert hardly ever spent time experimenting in a laboratory. All he needed was a pencil, paper, and his incredible imagination to come up with ideas.

Albert called the way he worked "thought experiments." For instance, because no one can actually travel at the speed of light, Albert simply imagined himself traveling on a beam of light. He pictured, in his mind, what would happen if he moved through space at 186,000 miles per second. Thought experiments helped him to understand many secrets of the universe.

When Albert first wrote about his ideas, they were **theories**. A theory is a logical explanation for something that can be tested through experiments. Sometimes theories are proven to be right. But sometimes they're wrong. Today, many of Albert's theories have been shown to be correct. For example, we now know for sure that **atoms** and **molecules** really exist, that **gravity** can bend light, and that time appears to slow down the faster you travel at very high speeds. It has also been proven, as Albert thought, that there is an incredible amount of energy in the tiny atoms that make up everything in the universe.

Albert Einstein was known for his wonderful sense of humor.

Albert Einstein was a pretty cool guy. Even though he dealt with very serious subjects, he always had a good sense of humor. He usually wore the same old, rumpled suit. He didn't like to wear socks, either. He made people feel comfortable and they enjoyed being around him.

Soon after Albert was born, his mother and father moved from Ulm to Munich, Germany. Mr. and Mrs. Einstein were worried about their son because he was born with an unusually large head. Albert didn't seem to be interested in learning to talk, either.

When Albert was two years old, his sister, Maja, was born. Albert remembered being disappointed because Maja didn't come with wheels. He thought she was a toy! But over the years, Maja became Albert's best friend.

Albert and his sister Maja in 1885

Albert and Maja were pretty happy as children. Mrs. Einstein provided violin lessons for both of them. At first, Albert hated taking lessons. As an adult, though, Albert loved playing the violin. It helped him to relax during breaks from his thought experiments.

Albert became fascinated with magnetism when his father gave him a compass.

When Albert was five years old, something happened that changed his life forever. His father gave him a **compass**. Albert was amazed! No matter which way he turned the compass, its needle would always move toward the north. At that moment, Albert's curiosity about the wonder of science and nature was sparked.

Albert knew there had to be mysterious, magnificent, hidden forces that controlled the way things in the world worked. He couldn't wait to find out what those forces were. In school, Albert's curiosity helped him become an excellent student in math and science. The problem was that he would study only subjects that interested him.

Albert (front row, third from right) in a class photograph in the early 1890s

Albert's teachers were often upset with him. They thought he was a wiseguy and tried forcing him to follow school rules. Soon Albert began to really dislike going to school. He started studying more on his own. With encouragement from his family and friends, Albert pretty much taught himself algebra and geometry by the time he was thirteen.

When Albert was fifteen, his father was offered a new job, and the family moved to Milan, Italy. Albert was left behind in Munich to finish high school. He was miserable. By now, he knew more about science and math than his teachers did. He was so bored and upset that he decided to quit school. His teachers and principal were glad to see him go.

Albert Einstein at about age 14

In 1895, sixteen-year-old Albert surprised his parents by showing up in Italy and letting them know he had quit school. They weren't happy with their son's decision. Even so, Albert did what he wanted to do. He spent days hiking all over the beautiful Italian countryside. He had time to collect ideas and thoughts about nature that would later lead to important experiments.

After a few months, his parents convinced him to finish high school so that he'd be able to get into college. They sent him a school in Switzerland. In 1896, Albert finished high school and entered the Swiss Federal Institute of Technology in Zurich.

As a teenager, Albert loved hiking through the Italian Alps (above).

The Swiss Institute of Technology was a great place to learn physics. Albert hoped to be a physics and math teacher some day. It wasn't long, though, before Albert got back to his old habits. He started skipping classes and studied only the subjects he liked.

Albert studied physics at the Swiss Institute of Technology in Zurich, Switzerland (above).

Albert (on the right) and his friend Marcel Grossmann

Albert began to get a reputation as a goof-off who didn't respect his teachers. Luckily for Albert, when it was time for final exams, he got help from his friend and classmate Marcel Grossmann. Marcel supplied notes that contained the information Albert had missed by skipping class. Albert carefully studied the notes and managed to pass his exams. He graduated from the Swiss Institute in 1900. Albert had a hard time finding a teaching job, though. None of his professors would write him a letter of recommendation!

Mileva Maríc was the only female student at the Swiss Federal Institute of Technology when Albert met her in 1896. Albert and Mileva married in 1903.

Even though the professors at the Swiss Institute of Technology hadn't cared for Albert's attitude, he had made lots of friends there. One was a student named Mileva Maríc. Mileva was very smart, too. She and Albert enjoyed spending hours together talking about math, science, and music.

Albert and Mileva decided to get married as soon as Albert could make enough money to support them. Albert was worried, though. He just couldn't find a job. Then his old friend, Marcel Grossmann, came to the rescue again. Marcel helped Albert get a job at the Swiss **Patent** Office, a place where inventors applied for patents. A patent is a document that gives an inventor complete control over the **manufacture** and sale of his or her invention.

Albert looks at a reference book while working in the patent office in Bern, Switzerland.

The patent office was the perfect place for Albert. He enjoyed looking over plans for new inventions. If he thought they would work, and were original, Albert would issue a patent. Albert also liked his job because he wasn't that busy. He had a lot of spare time to do what he had always wanted, which was to think about solving mysteries of the universe.

Mileva, Hans Albert, and Albert Einstein in 1904

Soon after Albert started his new job, he and Mileva got married. In 1904, their first son, Hans, was born. Albert could often be found at home, holding little Hans in one arm while writing tons of mathematical formulas with the other. Sometimes Albert was so wrapped up in writing his theories that he hardly noticed he had a new baby!

Eduard, Mileva, and Hans Albert in 1914

Albert and Mileva later had a second son. His name was Eduard. Unfortunately, Albert spent so much time concentrating on his work that Mileva sometimes felt ignored.

Even though things weren't going so well at home, Albert came up with some of his greatest ideas during this time. In 1905, Albert wrote a number of articles and sent them to a science magazine. The articles explained Albert's theories about what light is made of and how it travels from place to place.

Albert then gave evidence that atoms and molecules, the tiny particles that make up all things, actually existed. Before this, scientists weren't really sure. Albert wrote another paper the same year that made new predictions about space and time. If that weren't enough, Albert went on to come up with the most famous equation ever written, $E=mc^2$.

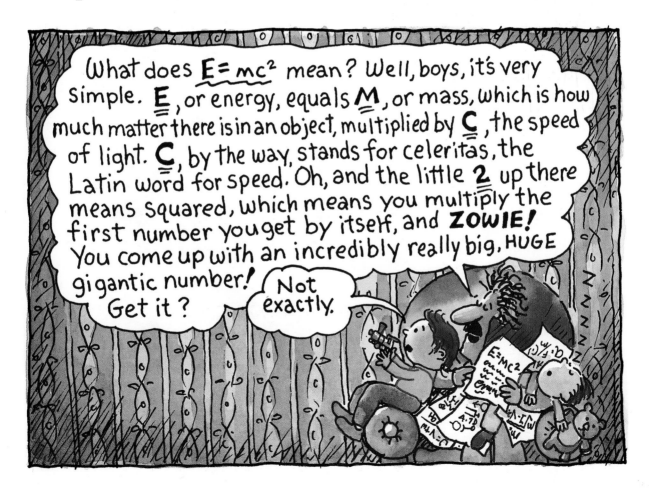

It's very hard to explain what this equation means. It sort of means that there is an incredibly huge amount of energy, even in very small amounts of matter.

Albert Einstein's theories weren't the easiest things to understand. Even many scientists, not to mention regular people, had a hard time figuring out exactly what Albert meant.

To top things off, a few years later, Albert wrote another amazing paper. He wrote that planets didn't orbit the sun in an exact, orderly way, controlled by the sun's gravity. Instead, Albert suggested that space was warped or curved, almost like the hilly surface of a skateboard park. He believed that stars moved and planets orbited the sun by following the curved paths of space. Scientists around the world were flipped out by Albert's ideas! Albert's General Theory of Relativity changed the way people had thought about the universe for hundreds of years.

Albert writes an equation on the blackboard during a lecture at the California Institute of Technology in 1931.

One incredible thing about Albert's theories was that he came up with them in his spare time, while working at the patent office. Albert didn't work there for long, though. As soon as scientists around the world began to understand Einstein's theories, Albert started getting job offers from lots of universities. Over the years, Albert taught and lectured at several different universities around the world.

Students always packed Albert's lecture halls to hear him speak. Albert tried to explain his complicated theories as simply as possible. He often used his sense of humor to relax students and keep their attention. And as busy as he was, Albert told his students to drop by his office any time if they had questions about their homework.

Albert traveling on a train with his second wife, Elsa, in 1955

Over the years, Albert and Mileva had grown further and further apart. In 1919, Albert divorced Mileva. He soon remarried. His new wife, Elsa, always protected Albert from pesty news reporters and curious fans. She wanted to make sure nothing interfered with her husband's work.

Albert Einstein's theories led to new branches of science and physics. Rocket scientists and astronauts have a better idea of what to expect when they travel into space because of Albert's predictions.

Albert was not involved with the development of the **atomic bomb**. But his equation, $E=mc^2$, led scientists to find a way to release incredible amounts of energy from atoms. In the 1930s, they made use of Einstein's theory by using machines to break apart atoms. This work led to the creation of the atomic bomb. In 1945, this bomb—the world's most powerful weapon—was used for the first time. Albert was terribly saddened that his idea was used for such a destructive purpose.

Scientists used information they learned from Einstein's theories to create the atomic bomb. Einstein was against the building of such a bomb and refused to work on the project. In 1945, the United States used this terrible weapon on Japan (above) to end World War II.

When German dictator Adolf Hitler (right) came to power in the early 1930s, Einstein left Germany, never to return.

Albert Einstein contributed more than scientific discoveries to the world. He was also known for working to prevent wars and for trying to stop countries from making atomic weapons. Albert lived through two horrible wars. Both of them were pretty much started by Germany, the country where he had been born. To Albert, the German government always seemed too anxious to send its armies into battle.

Albert proudly became U.S. citizen in 1940. Here he is shown during his citizenship ceremony, taking an oath of allegiance to the United States.

As a young man, Albert had been one of the few people living in Germany to let his antiwar feelings be known. In the early 1930s, **dictator** Adolf Hitler and his Nazi Party came to power in Germany. The Nazis hated Jewish people, and Albert came from a Jewish family. Albert's life was threatened and he decided he wanted to leave Germany. Fortunately, Albert was offered a job in the United States as a professor at The Institute for Advanced Study, in Princeton, New Jersey. Albert accepted the job and left Germany forever. He eventually became a citizen of the United States.

Albert Einstein spent the rest of his life doing research and thought experiments and working for world peace. He died in Princeton, New Jersey, in 1955, at the age of 76.

Einstein at home in 1954

Glossary

atom (AT-uhm) The tiniest part of a chemical element (such as oxygen) that has all the properties of that element; everything is made up of atoms

atomic bomb (uh-TOM-ik BOM) A powerful bomb whose explosion results from the energy that is released by splitting atoms

compass (KUHM-puhss) An instrument for finding directions; it has a needle that always points north

dictator (DIK-tay-tur) Someone who has complete control over a country

gravity (GRAV-uh-tee) The force of attraction between massive bodies in the universe, including the attraction of objects toward the center of the Earth

magnetism (MAG-nuh-tiz-im) A force, produced by a magnet or electric current, that pulls objects together or pushes them apart

manufacturing (man-yoo-FAK-chur-ing) The making of things in large amounts, often with the use of machinery

matter (MAT-ur) Anything that has weight and takes up space

molecule (MOL-uh-kyool) The smallest part of a substance (such as water) that has all the chemical properties of that substance; molecules are made up of more than one atom

patent (PAT-uhnt) A legal document giving an inventor the sole right to manufacture or sell an invention

physics (FIZ-iks) The science that deals with matter and energy

theory (THIHR-ee) A logical explanation, based on experimentation, that explains how or why something happens

Index